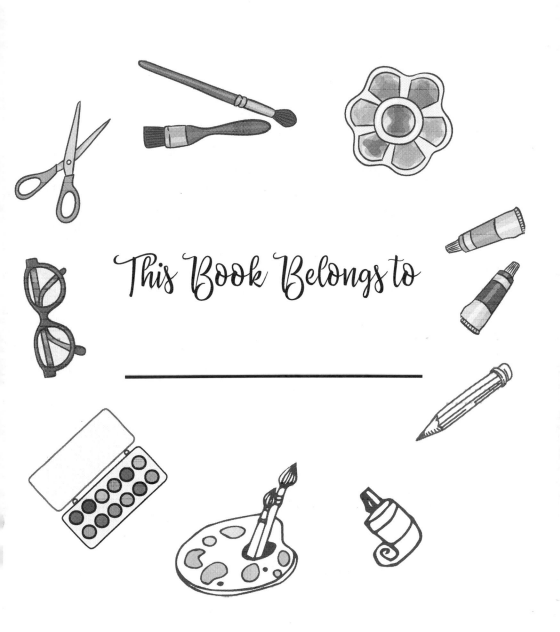

This Book Belongs to

_____

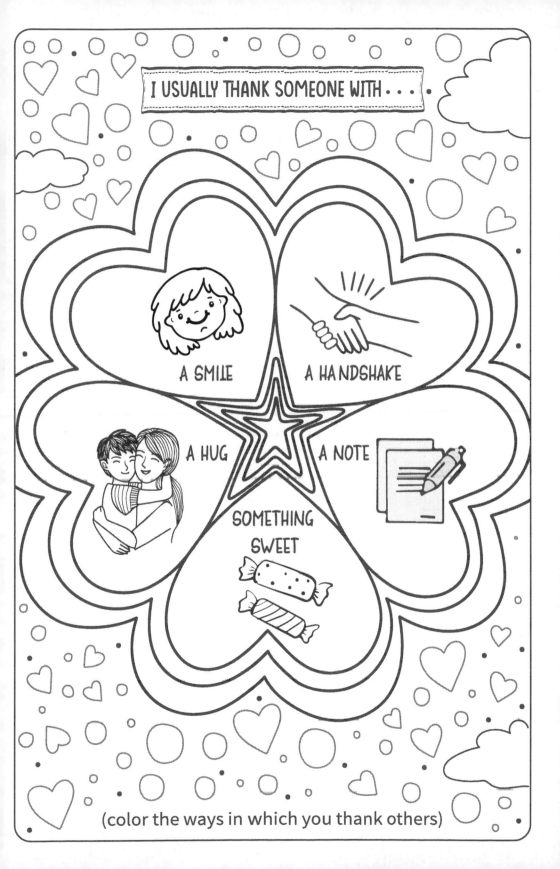

Date ___ / ___ / ___   <u>Sun</u>   <u>Mon</u>   <u>Tue</u>   <u>Wed</u>   <u>Thu</u>   <u>Fri</u>   <u>Sat</u>

TODAY I AM THANKFUL FOR

1. ....

2. ....

3. ....

SOMEONE WHO I THANKED TODAY ....

....

(Draw or write about
something you are good at)

DATE __ / __ / __ (Sun) (Mon) (Tue) (Wed) (Thu) (Fri) (Sat)

SOMETHING AWESOME THAT HAPPENED TODAY :

1. _____

2. _____

3. _____

TODAY I AM GRATEFUL FOR : _____

_____

HAPPINESS
SCALE

LAUGHTER IS THE KEY TO HAPPINESS

10
9
8
7
6
5
4
3
2
1

Ha haha.

(Draw or write about something
funny that happened this week)

DATE:
___ / ___ / ___

SUN MON TUE WED THU FRI SAT

I AM THANKFUL FOR TODAY
BECAUSE:

1.

2.

3.

EMOTIONS I FELT TODAY

THIS IS WHAT MY DAY LOOKED LIKE

(Draw or write about something that happened today)

SOMEONE WHO I THANKED TODAY:

SUN MON TUE WED THU FRI SAT ___/___/___ Date

SOMETHING GREAT THAT HAPPENED TODAY :

1. _____

2. _____

3. _____

SOMEONE WHO I THANKED TODAY : _____

_____

ACT OF GRATITUDE

HAPPINESS LEVEL

(Draw/ write about your today's
act of gratitude)

DATE ___ / ___ / ___

SUN   MON   TUE   WED   THU   FRI   SAT

SOMETHING AWESOME THAT HAPPENED TODAY :

1. _____

2. _____

3. _____

POSITIVE THOUGHT OF THE DAY :

TODAY I AM THANKFUL FOR :

Happiness Scale

8
7
9
6
10
5
4
3
2
1

(Write the names of the people you
are greatful for in the candies)

DATE __/__/__

SUN MON TUE WED THU FRI SAT

SOMETHING AWESOME THAT HAPPENED TODAY:

1. ....

2. ....

3. ....

EMOTIONS I FELT TODAY

TODAY I THANKED:

....

....

....

SOMETHING THAT INSPIRES ME

(Draw or write about something that inspires you)

(color the rays that have reasons you are grateful for)

DATE ___/___/___   SUN   MON   TUE   WED   THU   FRI   SAT

POSITIVE THOUGHT OF THE DAY :

I AM THANKFUL FOR TODAY BECAUSE :

1.

2.

3.

THIS IS WHAT MAKES MY LIFE EASIER

Happiness Scale

10
9
8
7
6
5
4
3
2
1

(Draw or write about something that makes your life easier)

DATE ___ / ___ / ___ SUN MON TUE WED THU FRI SAT

SOMETHING AWESOME THAT HAPPENED TODAY :

1. _____

2. _____

3. _____

EMOTIONS I FELT TODAY

SOMEONE WHO I THANKED TODAY : _____

_____

GOOD DEED OF THE WEEK :

Happiness Scale

7 8
9
6
10
5
4
3
2
1

(Name or Draw a good deed you did this week)

SUN MON TUE WED THU FRI SAT   DATE ___ / ___ / ___

TODAY I AM THANKFUL FOR:

1. _____

2. _____

3. _____

SOMEONE WHO I THANKED TODAY: _____

_____

HAPPINESS SCALE

TRUE KINDNESS LIES IN THE ACT OF GIVING

10
9
8
7
6
5
4
3
2
1

(Draw something that you would give someone to make them smile)

sun   MON   TUE   WED   THU   Fri   Sat

I AM THANKFUL FOR TODAY BECAUSE :

1. _____

2. _____

3. _____

— — · — POSITIVE THOUGHT OF THE DAY — · — ·· —

HAPPINESS LEVEL

(Draw or write about something that you like to share)

Date ___ / ___ / ___   <u>Sun</u>   <u>Mon</u>   <u>Tue</u>   <u>Wed</u>   <u>Thu</u>   <u>Fri</u>   <u>Sat</u>

TODAY I AM THANKFUL FOR

1.

2.

3.

SOMEONE WHO I THANKED TODAY

HAPPINESS
LEVEL

(Draw or write about
something you are good at)

DATE __ / __ / __ (Sun) (Mon) (Tue) (Wed) (Thu) (Fri) (Sat)

SOMETHING AWESOME THAT HAPPENED TODAY :

1. _____

2. _____

3. _____

TODAY I AM GRATEFUL FOR : _____

_____

HAPPINESS SCALE

LAUGHTER IS THE KEY TO HAPPINESS

10
9
8
7
6
5
4
3
2
1

Ha haha.

(Draw or write about something funny that happened this week)

(Find and circle the words of Gratitude)

```
S A R D Z D R E O A P I A N S H I N Q K A Y Z T
T Z L Y I A T P A Y U Y G Y B L W A Y E O C S F
H I C C C P L Y H L I K V A T E T S X N N B Y E
A E U O J P T G S I W T Y Z A M Q S E C A O F G
N B L W Q R I G G M Z R A A V U T D D O E F R O
K W H T R E S I R A B V Q D X I H O S U T L I O
F F K Z M C Q S O F S J U N D X A T H R Y W E D
U J L Z E I I X S S T R M W V G N R A A T P N O
L U N Y E A T H O U G H T F U L K S P G H T D O
I O L A A T C X J O Y A T E R E S I P E E C S G
A B H Y S E O H Y I R D T X Q B G T I K F E H G
C Q S G E O M E K F H R R G X Y I K N P Z P I R
K C D A E M P B D U X V U T Q T V H E S N S P A
N E O Q W Y A Y C Z K M K I S G I B S E C E S T
O C H Y Q D S J C O M P L I M E N T S X P R K E
W L I Y O U S V A A S S B P N Z G X M C S S F F
L N N D G K I S Y D V O B U N T E E T I N G G U
E A E L S B O Y I E K C A R I N G Y O T D G D L
D F S F O H N Y Z K R T Q L L V K L L E E C O T
G M Y K I N D N E S S G T O U X S K D D G G Q K
E X Y I T Z F Z Y Y M V J V D F I E F T A E I U
Z V K U C E Z Z V L H L K I F J U T X N G E J M
O C I S K V V F K K W T R N R D J I Z J N K L C
S Y I N T M U A M D R B Q G K J R C Y A E R M W
```

EXCITED	JOY	GOOD	LOVING
HAPPINESS	CARING	THOUGHTFUL	GRATEFUL
COMPLIMENT	ACKNOWLEDGE	KINDNESS	THANKSGIVING
THANKFUL	COMPASSION	ENCOURAGE	APPRECIATE

DATE:
___/___/___

Sun Mon Tue Wed Thu Fri Sat

I AM THANKFUL FOR TODAY BECAUSE:

1.

2.

3.

EMOTIONS I FELT TODAY

THIS IS WHAT MY DAY LOOKED LIKE

(Draw or write about something that happened today)

SOMEONE WHO I THANKED TODAY:

SOMETHING GREAT THAT HAPPENED TODAY :

1. _____

2. _____

3. _____

SOMEONE WHO I THANKED TODAY : _____

_____

ACT OF GRATITUDE

HAPPINESS LEVEL

(Draw/ write about your today's
act of gratitude)

DATE ___/___/___

SUN MON TUE WED THU FRI SAT

SOMETHING AWESOME THAT HAPPENED TODAY :

1.

2.

3.

POSITIVE THOUGHT OF THE DAY :

TODAY I AM THANKFUL FOR :

Happiness Scale

8
7
9
6
10
5
4
3
2
1

(Write the names of the people you
are greatful for in the candies)

DATE ___/___/___

SUN MON TUE WED THU FRI SAT

SOMETHING AWESOME THAT HAPPENED TODAY :

1. _____

2. _____

3. _____

EMOTIONS I FELT TODAY

TODAY I THANKED :

_____

_____

_____

— · — · — SOMETHING THAT INSPIRES ME — · · — · ·

(Draw or write about something that inspires you)

DATE ___/___/___   SUN MON TUE WED THU FRI SAT

POSITIVE THOUGHT OF THE DAY :

I AM THANKFUL FOR TODAY BECAUSE :

1.

2.

3.

THIS IS WHAT MAKES MY LIFE EASIER

Happiness Scale

10
9
8
7
6
5
4
3
2
1

(Draw or write about something that makes your life easier)

DATE ___ / ___ / ___ SUN MON TUE WED THU FRI SAT

SOMETHING AWESOME THAT HAPPENED TODAY :

1. _____

_____

2. _____

_____

3. _____

SOMEONE WHO I THANKED TODAY : _____

_____

EMOTIONS I FELT TODAY

GOOD DEED OF THE WEEK :

Happiness Scale

7 8
9
6
10
5
4
3
2
1

(Name or Draw a good deed you did this week)

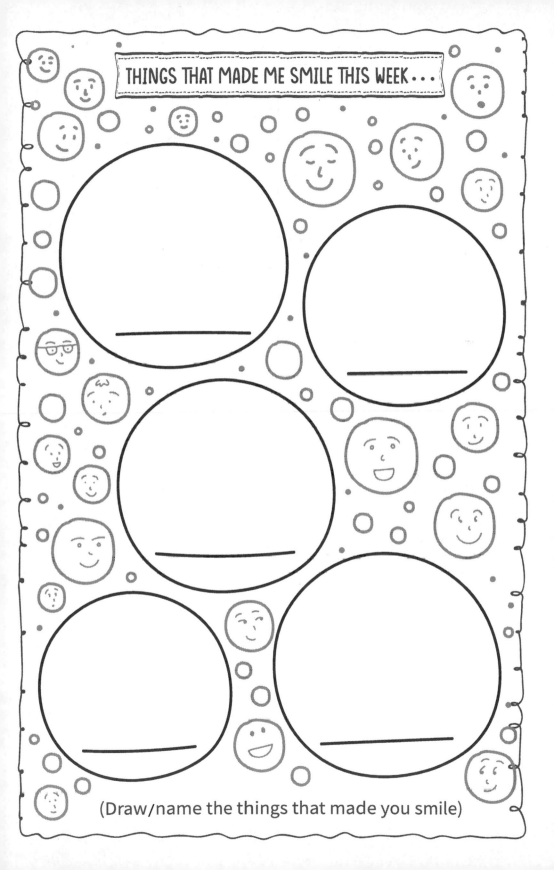

THINGS THAT MADE ME SMILE THIS WEEK...

(Draw/name the things that made you smile)

SUN MON TUE WED THU FRI SAT DATE ___/___/___

TODAY I AM THANKFUL FOR:

1. _____

2. _____

3. _____

SOMEONE WHO I THANKED TODAY: _____

_____

HAPPINESS SCALE

TRUE KINDNESS LIES IN THE ACT OF GIVING

10
9
8
7
6
5
4
3
2
1

(Draw something that you would give someone to make them smile)

DATE

___/___/___

I AM THANKFUL FOR TODAY BECAUSE :

1. _____

2. _____

3. _____

— — · — POSITIVE THOUGHT OF THE DAY — · — ·· —

HAPPINESS LEVEL

(Draw or write about something that you like to share)

Date ___ / ___ / ___   <u>Sun</u>   <u>Mon</u>   <u>Tue</u>   <u>Wed</u>   <u>Thu</u>   <u>Fri</u>   <u>Sat</u>

TODAY I AM THANKFUL FOR

1. _____

2. _____

3. _____

SOMEONE WHO I THANKED TODAY _____

_____

(Draw or write about
something you are good at)

DATE __/__/__   Sun Mon Tue Wed Thu Fri Sat

SOMETHING AWESOME THAT HAPPENED TODAY :

1. _____

2. _____

3. _____

TODAY I AM GRATEFUL FOR : _____

_____

HAPPINESS SCALE

LAUGHTER IS THE KEY TO HAPPINESS

10
9
8
7
6
5
4
3
2
1

Ha haha.

(Draw or write about something funny that happened this week)

DATE:
___ / ___ / ___

SUN MON TUE WED THU FRI SAT

I AM THANKFUL FOR TODAY BECAUSE:

1. _____

2. _____

3. _____

EMOTIONS I FELT TODAY

THIS IS WHAT MY DAY LOOKED LIKE

(Draw or write about something that happened today)

SOMEONE WHO I THANKED TODAY: _____

_____

sun mon Tue wed Thu Fri sat ___ / ___ / ___ Date

SOMETHING GREAT THAT HAPPENED TODAY :

1. _____

2. _____

3. _____

SOMEONE WHO I THANKED TODAY : _____

_____

ACT OF GRATITUDE

HAPPINESS LEVEL

(Draw/ write about your today's
act of gratitude)

I AM THANKFUL FOR MY FAMILY AND FRIENDS

(Draw & Color people who you are thankful for)

Date ___/___/___

SUN MON TUE WED THU FRI SAT

SOMETHING AWESOME THAT HAPPENED TODAY :

1. _____

2. _____

3. _____

— · · — POSITIVE THOUGHT OF THE DAY : —— · · —

Happiness Scale

TODAY I AM THANKFUL FOR :

(Write the names of the people you
are greatful for in the candies)

DATE __ / __ / __

SUN   MON   TUE   WED   THU   FRI   SAT

SOMETHING AWESOME THAT HAPPENED TODAY :

1. _____

2. _____

3. _____

EMOTIONS I FELT TODAY

TODAY I THANKED :

_____

_____

_____

SOMETHING THAT INSPIRES ME

(Draw or write about something that inspires you)

DATE ___ / ___ / ___   SUN   MON   TUE   WED   THU   FRI   SAT

POSITIVE THOUGHT OF THE DAY:

I AM THANKFUL FOR TODAY BECAUSE:

1.

2.

3.

THIS IS WHAT MAKES MY LIFE EASIER

Happiness Scale

10
9
8
7
6
5
4
3
2
1

(Draw or write about something that makes your life easier)

Date ___/___/___   Sun Mon Tue Wed Thu Fri Sat

SOMETHING AWESOME THAT HAPPENED TODAY :

1. _____

2. _____

3. _____

SOMEONE WHO I THANKED TODAY : _____

_____

EMOTIONS I FELT TODAY

GOOD DEED OF THE WEEK :

Happiness Scale

8
7
9
6
10
5
4
3
2
1

(Name or Draw a good deed you did this week)

Sun Mon Tue Wed Thu Fri Sat DATE __/__/__

TODAY I AM THANKFUL FOR:

1. _____

2. _____

3. _____

SOMEONE WHO I THANKED TODAY: _____

_____

HAPPINESS SCALE

TRUE KINDNESS LIES IN THE ACT OF GIVING

10
9
8
7
6
5
4
3
2
1

(Draw something that you would give someone to make them smile)

Sun   Mon   Tue   Wed   Thu   Fri   Sat

I AM THANKFUL FOR TODAY BECAUSE :

1. _____

2. _____

3. _____

— · — · — POSITIVE THOUGHT OF THE DAY — · — · · — · ·

HAPPINESS LEVEL

(Draw or write about something that you like to share)

I AM THANKFUL FOR THESE SWEET FRIENDS...

(Draw/name the sweet treats you are thankful for)

Date ___/___/___   Sun   Mon   Tue   Wed   Thu   Fri   Sat

TODAY I AM THANKFUL FOR

1. ....

2. ....

3. ....

SOMEONE WHO I THANKED TODAY ....

....

HAPPINESS
LEVEL

(Draw or write about
something you are good at)

DATE ___/___/___ (Sun) (Mon) (Tue) (Wed) (Thu) (Fri) (Sat)

SOMETHING AWESOME THAT HAPPENED TODAY :

1. _____

2. _____

3. _____

TODAY I AM GRATEFUL FOR : _____

_____

HAPPINESS SCALE

LAUGHTER IS THE KEY TO HAPPINESS

10
9
8
7
6
5
4
3
2
1

Ha haha.

(Draw or write about something funny that happened this week)

I AM THANKFUL FOR TODAY BECAUSE:

1. _____

_____

2. _____

_____

3. _____

EMOTIONS I FELT TODAY

THIS IS WHAT MY DAY LOOKED LIKE

(Draw or write about something that happened today)

SOMEONE WHO I THANKED TODAY: _____

_____

sun mon Tue wed Thu fri sat __/__/__ Date

SOMETHING GREAT THAT HAPPENED TODAY :

1. _____

2. _____

3. _____

SOMEONE WHO I THANKED TODAY : _____

_____

ACT OF GRATITUDE

HAPPINESS LEVEL

(Draw/ write about your today's
act of gratitude)

DATE ___/___/___   SUN MON TUE WED THU FRI SAT

SOMETHING AWESOME THAT HAPPENED TODAY :

1. _____

2. _____

3. _____

— POSITIVE THOUGHT OF THE DAY : —

Happiness Scale

8
7
9
6
10
5
4
3
2
1

TODAY I AM THANKFUL FOR :

(Write the names of the people you
are greatful for in the candies)

DATE _/_/_

SUN MON TUE WED THU FRI SAT

SOMETHING AWESOME THAT HAPPENED TODAY :

1. ....

2. ....

3. ....

EMOTIONS I FELT TODAY

TODAY I THANKED :

....

....

....

SOMETHING THAT INSPIRES ME

(Draw or write about something that inspires you)

I AM THANKFUL IN SUMMER FOR...

(What do you like about summer?
Draw/name them)

POSITIVE THOUGHT OF THE DAY :

I AM THANKFUL FOR TODAY BECAUSE :

1.

2.

3.

THIS IS WHAT MAKES MY LIFE EASIER

Happiness Scale

10
9
8
7
6
5
4
3
2
1

(Draw or write about something that makes your life easier)

Date ___ / ___ / ___ SUN MON TUE WED THU FRI SAT

SOMETHING AWESOME THAT HAPPENED TODAY :

1. _____

2. _____

3. _____

SOMEONE WHO I THANKED TODAY : _____

EMOTIONS I FELT TODAY

GOOD DEED OF THE WEEK :

Happiness Scale

7 8
9
6
10
5
4
3
2
1

(Name or Draw a good deed you did this week)

Sun Mon Tue Wed Thu Fri Sat   DATE ___ / ___ / ___

TODAY I AM THANKFUL FOR:

1. _____

2. _____

3. _____

SOMEONE WHO I THANKED TODAY: _____

_____

HAPPINESS SCALE

TRUE KINDNESS LIES IN THE ACT OF GIVING

10
9
8
7
6
5
4
3
2
1

(Draw something that you would give someone to make them smile)

Date:
___/___/___

I AM THANKFUL FOR TODAY BECAUSE :

1. _____

2. _____

3. _____

— — — · — POSITIVE THOUGHT OF THE DAY — · — ·· — ·· —

HAPPINESS LEVEL

(Draw or write about something that you like to share)

Date ___ / ___ / ___   <u>Sun</u>   <u>Mon</u>   <u>Tue</u>   <u>Wed</u>   <u>Thu</u>   <u>Fri</u>   <u>Sat</u>

TODAY I AM THANKFUL FOR

1.

2.

3.

SOMEONE WHO I THANKED TODAY

HAPPINESS
LEVEL

(Draw or write about
something you are good at)

DATE __ / __ / __   (SUN) (MON) (TUE) (WED) (THU) (FRI) (SAT)

SOMETHING AWESOME THAT HAPPENED TODAY :

1. _____

2. _____

3. _____

TODAY I AM GRATEFUL FOR : _____

_____

HAPPINESS
SCALE

LAUGHTER IS THE KEY TO HAPPINESS

10
9
8
7
6
5
4
3
2
1

Ha haha..

(Draw or write about something
funny that happened this week)

I AM THANKFUL IN WINTER FOR...

(What do you like about winter?
Draw/name them)

DATE:
___/___/___

SUN   MON   TUE   WED   THU   FRI   SAT

I AM THANKFUL FOR TODAY
BECAUSE:

EMOTIONS I FELT TODAY

1. _____

_____

2. _____

_____

3. _____

THIS IS WHAT MY DAY LOOKED LIKE

(Draw or write about something that happened today)

SOMEONE WHO I THANKED TODAY: _____

_____

SOMETHING GREAT THAT HAPPENED TODAY :

1. _____

2. _____

3. _____

SOMEONE WHO I THANKED TODAY : _____

_____

ACT OF GRATITUDE

HAPPINESS LEVEL

(Draw/ write about your today's
act of gratitude)

DATE __/__/__

SUN MON TUE WED THU FRI SAT

SOMETHING AWESOME THAT HAPPENED TODAY:

1. _____

2. _____

3. _____

— POSITIVE THOUGHT OF THE DAY: —

TODAY I AM THANKFUL FOR:

Happiness Scale

7 8 9 6 10 5 4 3 2 1

(Write the names of the people you are greatful for in the candies)

DATE ___/___/___

SUN MON TUE WED THU FRI SAT

SOMETHING AWESOME THAT HAPPENED TODAY :

1. _____

2. _____

3. _____

EMOTIONS I FELT TODAY

TODAY I THANKED :

_____

_____

_____

SOMETHING THAT INSPIRES ME

(Draw or write about something that inspires you)

Date ___ / ___ / ___   (Sun) (Mon) (Tue) (Wed) (Thu) (Fri) (Sat)

— POSITIVE THOUGHT OF THE DAY : —

I AM THANKFUL FOR TODAY BECAUSE:

1.

2.

3.

THIS IS WHAT MAKES MY LIFE EASIER

Happiness Scale

10
9
8
7
6
5
4
3
2
1

(Draw or write about something that makes your life easier)

DATE ___/___/___ SUN MON TUE WED THU FRI SAT

SOMETHING AWESOME THAT HAPPENED TODAY :

1. _____

2. _____

3. _____

SOMEONE WHO I THANKED TODAY :

_____

EMOTIONS I FELT TODAY

GOOD DEED OF THE WEEK :

Happiness Scale

8
7
9
6
10
5
4
3
2
1

(Name or Draw a good deed you did this week)

I AM THANKFUL IN AUTUMN FOR...

(What do you like about autumn?
Draw/name them)

SUN   MON   TUE   WED   THU   FRI   SAT   DATE ___/___/___

TODAY I AM THANKFUL FOR:

1. _____

2. _____

3. _____

SOMEONE WHO I THANKED TODAY: _____

_____

HAPPINESS SCALE

TRUE KINDNESS LIES IN THE ACT OF GIVING

10
9
8
7
6
5
4
3
2
1

(Draw something that you would give someone to make them smile)

Sun   Mon   Tue   Wed   Thu   Fri   Sat

DATE
__ / __ / __

I AM THANKFUL FOR TODAY BECAUSE :

1. _____

2. _____

3. _____

— · — · · — POSITIVE THOUGHT OF THE DAY — · — · · — · ·

HAPPINESS LEVEL

(Draw or write about something that you like to share)

Date ___ / ___ / ___   <u>SUN</u>   <u>MON</u>   <u>TUE</u>   <u>WED</u>   <u>THU</u>   <u>FRI</u>   <u>SAT</u>

TODAY I AM THANKFUL FOR

1. _____

2. _____

3. _____

SOMEONE WHO I THANKED TODAY _____

_____

**HAPPINESS
LEVEL**

(Draw or write about
something you are good at)

DATE __ / __ / __ (SUN) (MON) (TUE) (WED) (THU) (FRI) (SAT)

SOMETHING AWESOME THAT HAPPENED TODAY :

1. _____

2. _____

3. _____

TODAY I AM GRATEFUL FOR : _____

_____

HAPPINESS SCALE

LAUGHTER IS THE KEY TO HAPPINESS

10
9
8
7
6
5
4
3
2
1

Ha haha..

(Draw or write about something
funny that happened this week)

DATE:
___/___/___

SUN   MON   TUE   WED   THU   FRI   SAT

I AM THANKFUL FOR TODAY BECAUSE:

1. _____

2. _____

_____

3. _____

EMOTIONS I FELT TODAY

THIS IS WHAT MY DAY LOOKED LIKE

(Draw or write about something that happened today)

SOMEONE WHO I THANKED TODAY: _____

_____

Sun Mon Tue Wed Thu Fri Sat ___ / ___ / ___ Date

SOMETHING GREAT THAT HAPPENED TODAY :

1.

2.

3.

SOMEONE WHO I THANKED TODAY : _____

ACT OF GRATITUDE

HAPPINESS LEVEL

(Draw/ write about your today's act of gratitude)

DATE ___ / ___ / ___

SUN MON TUE WED THU FRI SAT

SOMETHING AWESOME THAT HAPPENED TODAY :

1. _____

2. _____

3. _____

POSITIVE THOUGHT OF THE DAY :

Happiness Scale

8
7
9
6
10
5
4
3
2
1

TODAY I AM THANKFUL FOR :

(Write the names of the people you
are greatful for in the candies)

DATE __/__/__

SUN MON TUE WED THU FRI SAT

SOMETHING AWESOME THAT HAPPENED TODAY:

1. ....

2. ....

3. ....

EMOTIONS I FELT TODAY

TODAY I THANKED:

....

....

....

— SOMETHING THAT INSPIRES ME —

(Draw or write about something that inspires you)

DATE ___/___/___ {SUN} {MON} {TUE} {WED} {THU} {FRI} {SAT}

— · — · — POSITIVE THOUGHT OF THE DAY : — · · — · ·

I AM THANKFUL FOR TODAY BECAUSE:

1.

2.

3.

THIS IS WHAT MAKES MY LIFE EASIER

Happiness Scale

10
9
8
7
6
5
4
3
2
1

(Draw or write about something that makes your life easier)

SOMETHING AWESOME THAT
HAPPENED TODAY :

1. _____

2. _____

3. _____

SOMEONE WHO I THANKED TODAY : _____

_____

EMOTIONS I FELT TODAY

GOOD DEED OF THE WEEK :

Happiness Scale

7 8
9
6
10
5
4
3
2
1

(Name or Draw a good deed you did this week)

Sun Mon Tue Wed Thu Fri Sat   DATE ___ / ___ / ___

TODAY I AM THANKFUL FOR:

1. _____

2. _____

3. _____

SOMEONE WHO I THANKED TODAY: _____

_____

HAPPINESS SCALE

TRUE KINDNESS LIES IN THE
ACT OF GIVING

10
9
8
7
6
5
4
3
2
1

(Draw something that you would
give someone to make them smile)

Sun   Mon   Tue   Wed   Thu   Fri   Sat

DATE

___/___/___

I AM THANKFUL FOR TODAY BECAUSE :

1.

2.

3.

——·——··——POSITIVE THOUGHT OF THE DAY——·——··——··

HAPPINESS LEVEL

(Draw or write about something that you like to share)

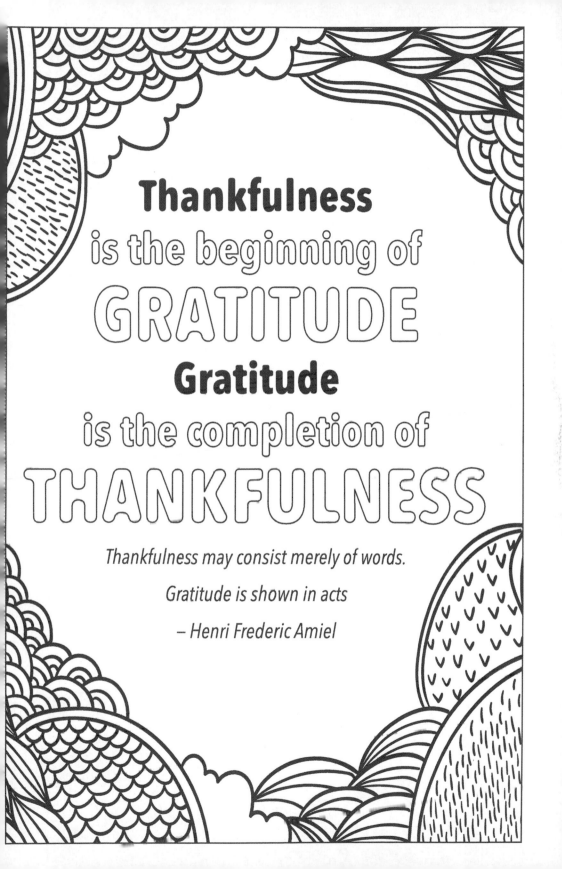

Thankfulness
is the beginning of
GRATITUDE
Gratitude
is the completion of
THANKFULNESS

Thankfulness may consist merely of words.

Gratitude is shown in acts

– Henri Frederic Amiel

Date ___ / ___ / ___ <u>Sun</u> <u>Mon</u> <u>Tue</u> <u>Wed</u> <u>Thu</u> <u>Fri</u> <u>Sat</u>

TODAY I AM THANKFUL FOR

1. _____

2. _____

3. _____

SOMEONE WHO I THANKED TODAY _____

_____

HAPPINESS
LEVEL

(Draw or write about
something you are good at)

DATE ___ / ___ / ___   SUN   MON   TUE   WED   THU   FRI   SAT

SOMETHING AWESOME THAT HAPPENED TODAY :

1. _____

2. _____

3. _____

TODAY I AM GRATEFUL FOR : _____

_____

HAPPINESS SCALE

10
9
8
7
6
5
4
3
2
1

LAUGHTER IS THE KEY TO HAPPINESS

Ha haha..

(Draw or write about something funny that happened this week)

DATE:

___/___/___

Sun   Mon   Tue   Wed   Thu   Fri   Sat

I AM THANKFUL FOR TODAY BECAUSE:

1. _____

_____

2. _____

_____

3. _____

EMOTIONS I FELT TODAY

THIS IS WHAT MY DAY LOOKED LIKE

(Draw or write about something that happened today)

SOMEONE WHO I THANKED TODAY: _____

_____

SOMETHING GREAT THAT HAPPENED TODAY :

1. _____

2. _____

3. _____

SOMEONE WHO I THANKED TODAY : _____

_____

ACT OF GRATITUDE

HAPPINESS LEVEL

(Draw/ write about your today's
act of gratitude)

DATE ___/___/___

SUN MON TUE WED THU FRI SAT

SOMETHING AWESOME THAT HAPPENED TODAY :

1. _____

2. _____

3. _____

— POSITIVE THOUGHT OF THE DAY : —

Happiness Scale

10
9
8
7
6
5
4
3
2
1

TODAY I AM THANKFUL FOR :

(Write the names of the people you are greatful for in the candies)

DATE ___/___/___

Sun Mon Tue Wed Thu Fri Sat

SOMETHING AWESOME THAT HAPPENED TODAY:

1. ....

2. ....

3. ....

EMOTIONS I FELT TODAY

TODAY I THANKED:

....

....

....

— — — · — SOMETHING THAT INSPIRES ME — · · — · · —

(Draw or write about something that inspires you)

DATE ____ / ____ / ____   Sun Mon Tue Wed Thu Fri Sat

— POSITIVE THOUGHT OF THE DAY : —

I AM THANKFUL FOR TODAY BECAUSE :

1.

2.

3.

THIS IS WHAT MAKES MY LIFE EASIER

Happiness Scale

10
9
8
7
6
5
4
3
2
1

(Draw or write about something that makes your life easier)

SOMETHING AWESOME THAT HAPPENED TODAY :

1. _____

2. _____

3. _____

SOMEONE WHO I THANKED TODAY : _____

_____

EMOTIONS I FELT TODAY

GOOD DEED OF THE WEEK :

Happiness Scale

7 8
9
6
10
5
4
3
2
1

(Name or Draw a good deed you did this week)

Sun Mon Tue Wed Thu Fri Sat DATE ___/___/___

TODAY I AM THANKFUL FOR:

1. _____

2. _____

3. _____

SOMEONE WHO I THANKED TODAY: _____

_____

HAPPINESS SCALE

TRUE KINDNESS LIES IN THE ACT OF GIVING

10
9
8
7
6
5
4
3
2
1

(Draw something that you would give someone to make them smile)

I AM THANKFUL FOR TODAY BECAUSE :

1.

2.

3.

— · — · — POSITIVE THOUGHT OF THE DAY — · — · · — · ·

HAPPINESS LEVEL

(Draw or write about something that you like to share)

Date ___/___/___   Sun   Mon   Tue   Wed   Thu   Fri   Sat

TODAY I AM THANKFUL FOR

1. _____

2. _____

3. _____

SOMEONE WHO I THANKED TODAY _____

_____

(Draw or write about
something you are good at)

DATE __/__/__   SUN   MON   TUE   WED   THU   FRI   SAT

SOMETHING AWESOME THAT HAPPENED TODAY :

1.

2.

3.

TODAY I AM GRATEFUL FOR : _____

HAPPINESS
SCALE

LAUGHTER IS THE KEY TO HAPPINESS

10
9
8
7
6
5
4
3
2
1

Ha haha..

(Draw or write about something
funny that happened this week)

DATE:
____/____/____

SUN   MON   TUE   WED   THU   FRI   SAT

I AM THANKFUL FOR TODAY BECAUSE:

1. _____

_____

2. _____

_____

3. _____

EMOTIONS I FELT TODAY

THIS IS WHAT MY DAY LOOKED LIKE

(Draw or write about something that happened today)

SOMEONE WHO I THANKED TODAY: _____

_____

SOMETHING GREAT THAT HAPPENED TODAY :

1. _____

2. _____

3. _____

SOMEONE WHO I THANKED TODAY : _____

_____

ACT OF GRATITUDE

HAPPINESS LEVEL

(Draw/ write about your today's
act of gratitude)

DATE __/__/__

SUN MON TUE WED THU FRI SAT

SOMETHING AWESOME THAT HAPPENED TODAY :

1. _____

2. _____

3. _____

— · — · — POSITIVE THOUGHT OF THE DAY : — · · — · ·

Happiness Scale

8 9 9 10 6 5 4 3 2 1

TODAY I AM THANKFUL FOR :

(Write the names of the people you are greatful for in the candies)

DATE __/__/__

SUN MON TUE WED THU FRI SAT

SOMETHING AWESOME THAT HAPPENED TODAY:

1. _____

2. _____

3. _____

EMOTIONS I FELT TODAY

TODAY I THANKED:

_____

_____

_____

— · — · — SOMETHING THAT INSPIRES ME — ·· — ··

(Draw or write about something that inspires you)

DATE ___ / ___ / ___   SUN MON TUE WED THU FRI SAT

POSITIVE THOUGHT OF THE DAY :

I AM THANKFUL FOR TODAY BECAUSE :

1.

2.

3.

THIS IS WHAT MAKES MY LIFE EASIER

Happiness Scale

10
9
8
7
6
5
4
3
2
1

(Draw or write about something that makes your life easier)

SOMETHING AWESOME THAT HAPPENED TODAY :

1. _____

2. _____

3. _____

SOMEONE WHO I THANKED TODAY : _____

EMOTIONS I FELT TODAY

GOOD DEED OF THE WEEK :

Happiness Scale

(Name or Draw a good deed you did this week)

Sun Mon Tue Wed Thu Fri Sat DATE ___/___/___

TODAY I AM THANKFUL FOR:

1. _____

2. _____

3. _____

SOMEONE WHO I THANKED TODAY: _____

_____

HAPPINESS SCALE

TRUE KINDNESS LIES IN THE ACT OF GIVING

10
9
8
7
6
5
4
3
2
1

(Draw something that you would give someone to make them smile)

Sun   Mon   Tue   Wed   Thu   Fri   Sat

DATE
___/___/___

I AM THANKFUL FOR TODAY BECAUSE :

1. ....

2. ....

3. ....

— · — · · — POSITIVE THOUGHT OF THE DAY — · — · · — · ·

HAPPINESS LEVEL

(Draw or write about something that you like to share)

Date ____ / ____ / ____   <u>Sun</u>   <u>Mon</u>   <u>Tue</u>   <u>Wed</u>   <u>Thu</u>   <u>Fri</u>   <u>Sat</u>

TODAY I AM THANKFUL FOR

1. _____

2. _____

3. _____

SOMEONE WHO I THANKED TODAY _____

_____

HAPPINESS
LEVEL

(Draw or write about
something you are good at)

DATE ___/___/___   SUN   MON   TUE   WED   THU   FRI   SAT

SOMETHING AWESOME THAT HAPPENED TODAY :

1.

2.

3.

TODAY I AM GRATEFUL FOR : _____

_____

HAPPINESS SCALE

LAUGHTER IS THE KEY TO HAPPINESS

10
9
8
7
6
5
4
3
2
1

Ha haha.

(Draw or write about something funny that happened this week)

DATE:
___ / ___ / ___

sun Mon Tue Wed Thu Fri sat

I AM THANKFUL FOR TODAY BECAUSE:

1. _____

_____

2. _____

_____

3. _____

EMOTIONS I FELT TODAY

THIS IS WHAT MY DAY LOOKED LIKE

(Draw or write about something that happened today)

SOMEONE WHO I THANKED TODAY: _____

_____

SOMETHING GREAT THAT HAPPENED TODAY :

1.

2.

3.

SOMEONE WHO I THANKED TODAY :

ACT OF GRATITUDE

HAPPINESS LEVEL

(Draw/ write about your today's
act of gratitude)

DAte ___/___/___

SUN MON TUE WED THU FRI SAT

SOMETHING AWESOME THAT HAPPENED TODAY :

1. _____

2. _____

3. _____

— — — POSITIVE THOUGHT OF THE DAY : — · — ·· —

Happiness Scale

7 8
9
6
10
5
4
3
2
1

TODAY I AM THANKFUL FOR :

(Write the names of the people you are greatful for in the candies)

DATE _ _ / _ _ / _ _

SUN MON TUE WED THU FRI SAT

SOMETHING AWESOME THAT HAPPENED TODAY :

1. ....

2. ....

3. ....

EMOTIONS I FELT TODAY

TODAY I THANKED :

....

....

....

- - - - · - - SOMETHING THAT INSPIRES ME - — · · — · ·

(Draw or write about something that inspires you)

Date ____ / ____ / ____   (Sun) (Mon) (Tue) (Wed) (Thu) (Fri) (Sat)

POSITIVE THOUGHT OF THE DAY:

I AM THANKFUL FOR TODAY BECAUSE:

1. _____

2. _____

3. _____

THIS IS WHAT MAKES MY LIFE EASIER

Happiness Scale

10
9
8
7
6
5
4
3
2
1

(Draw or write about something that makes your life easier)

DATE __ __ / __ __ / __ __ SUN MON TUE WED THU FRI SAT

SOMETHING AWESOME THAT HAPPENED TODAY :

1. _____

2. _____

3. _____

SOMEONE WHO I THANKED TODAY : _____

_____

EMOTIONS I FELT TODAY

GOOD DEED OF THE WEEK :

Happiness Scale

8
7
9
6
10
5
4
3
2
1

(Name or Draw a good deed you did this week)

TAG YOUR FRIENDS

Use the space to tag yourself & your friends & let the fun begin.

THE MAD

THE FODDIE

THE DORK

LEFT

- analysis
- logic
- facts
- sequencing
- mathematics
- language

RIGHT

- creativity
- intuition
- feelings
- imagination
- daydreaming
- arts

Facts about Brain

Made in the USA
Middletown, DE
12 November 2021

52206862R00068